Wild Apples

by Henry David Thoreau

APPLEWOOD BOOKS
CAMBRIDGE
1989

Wild Apples was originally published in
The Atlantic Monthly, November 1862.

ISBN: 1-55709-130-7

Thank you for purchasing an Applewood Book.
Applewood reprints America's lively
classics—books from the past which are still of
interest to modern readers—subjects such as
cooking, gardening, money, travel, nature, sports,
and history. Applewood Books are distributed by
The Globe Pequot Press of Chester, CT. For a free
copy of our current catalog, please write to Applewood Books, c/o The Globe Pequot Press, 138
West Main Street, Chester, CT 06412.

10 9 8 7 6 5 4 3 2

WILD APPLES.

(1862.)

THE HISTORY OF THE APPLE-TREE.

It is remarkable how closely the history of the Apple-tree is connected with that of man. The geologist tells us that the order of the *Rosaceæ*, which includes the Apple, also the true Grasses, and the *Labiatæ*, or Mints, were introduced only a short time previous to the appearance of man on the globe.

It appears that apples made a part of the food of that unknown primitive people whose traces have lately been found at the bottom of the Swiss lakes, supposed to be older than the foundation of Rome, so old that they had no metallic implements. An entire black and shrivelled Crab-Apple has been recovered from their stores.

Tacitus says of the ancient Germans, that they satisfied their hunger with wild apples (*agrestia poma*) among other things.

Niebuhr observes that " the words for a house,

a field, a plough, ploughing, wine, oil, milk, sheep, apples, and others relating to agriculture and the gentler way of life, agree in Latin and Greek, while the Latin words for all objects pertaining to war or the chase are utterly alien from the Greek." Thus the apple-tree may be considered a symbol of peace no less than the olive.

The apple was early so important, and generally distributed, that its name traced to its root in many languages signifies fruit in general. Μῆλον, in Greek, means an apple, also the fruit of other trees, also a sheep and any cattle, and finally riches in general.

The apple-tree has been celebrated by the Hebrews, Greeks, Romans, and Scandinavians. Some have thought that the first human pair were tempted by its fruit. Goddesses are fabled to have contended for it, dragons were set to watch it, and heroes were employed to pluck it.

The tree is mentioned in at least three places in the Old Testament, and its fruit in two or three more. Solomon sings, — "As the apple-tree among the trees of the wood, so is my beloved among the sons." And again, — "Stay me with flagons, comfort me with apples." The noblest part of man's noblest feature is named from this fruit, "the apple of the eye."

The apple-tree is also mentioned ·by Homer

and Herodotus. Ulysses saw in the glorious garden of Alcinoüs "pears and pomegranates, and apple-trees bearing beautiful fruit" (καὶ μηλέαι ἀγλαόκαρποι). And according to Homer, apples were among the fruits which Tantalus could not pluck, the wind ever blowing their boughs away from him. Theophrastus knew and described the apple-tree as a botanist.

According to the Prose Edda, "Iduna keeps in a box the apples which the gods, when they feel old age approaching, have only to taste of to become young again. It is in this manner that they will be kept in renovated youth until Ragnarök" (or the destruction of the gods).

I learn from Loudon that "the ancient Welsh bards were rewarded for excelling in song by the token of the apple-spray;" and "in the Highlands of Scotland the apple-tree is the badge of the clan Lamont."

The apple-tree (*Pyrus malus*) belongs chiefly to the northern temperate zone. Loudon says, that "it grows spontaneously in every part of Europe except the frigid zone, and throughout Western Asia, China, and Japan." We have also two or three varieties of the apple indigenous in North America. The cultivated apple-tree was first introduced into this country by the earliest settlers, and is thought to do as well or better here than anywhere else.

Probably some of the varieties which are now cultivated were first introduced into Britain by the Romans.

Pliny, adopting the distinction of Theophrastus, says,—" Of trees there are some which are altogether wild (*sylvestres*), some more civilized (*urbaniores*)." Theophrastus includes the apple among the last; and, indeed, it is in this sense the most civilized of al. trees. It is as harmless as a dove, as beautiful as a rose, and as valuable as flocks and herds. It has been longer cultivated than any other, and so is more humanized; and who knows but, like the dog, it will at length be no longer traceable to its wild original? It migrates with man, like the dog and horse and cow: first, perchance, from Greece to Italy, thence to England, thence to America; and our Western emigrant is still marching steadily toward the setting sun with the seeds of the apple in his pocket, or perhaps a few young trees strapped to his load. At least a million apple-trees are thus set farther westward this year than any cultivated ones grew last year. Consider how the Blossom-Week, like the Sabbath, is thus annually spreading over the prairies; for when man migrates, he carries with him not only his birds, quadrupeds, insects, vegetables, and his very sward, but his orchard also.

The leaves and tender twigs are an agreeable food to many domestic animals, as the cow, horse, sheep, and goat ; and the fruit is sought after by the first, as well as by the hog. Thus there appears to have existed a natural alliance between these animals and this tree from the first. " The fruit of the Crab in the forests of France " is said to be " a great resource for the wild-boar."

Not only the Indian, but many indigenous insects, birds, and quadrupeds, welcomed the apple-tree to these shores. The tent-caterpillar saddled her eggs on the very first twig that was formed, and it has since shared her affections with the wild cherry ; and the canker-worm also in a measure abandoned the elm to feed on it. As it grew apace, the bluebird, robin, cherry-bird, king-bird, and many more, came with haste and built their nests and warbled in its boughs, and so became orchard-birds, and multiplied more than ever. It was an era in the history of their race. The downy woodpecker found such a savory morsel under its bark, that he perforated it in a ring quite round the tree, before he left it, — a thing which he had never done before, to my knowledge. It did not take the partridge long to find out how sweet its buds were, and every winter eve she flew, and still flies, from the wood, to pluck them, much to the farmer's sorrow. The rabbit, too, was not slow to learn the taste of its twigs and bark; and when the fruit was ripe, the squirrel half-rolled, half-carried it to his hole; and even the musquash crept up the bank from the brook at evening, and greedily devoured it, until he had worn a path in the grass there; and when it was frozen and thawed, the crow and the jay were glad to taste it occasionally. The owl crept into the first apple-tree that became hollow, and fairly hooted with delight, finding it just the place for him; so, settling down into it, he has remained there ever since.

My theme being the Wild Apple, I will merely glance at some of the seasons in the annual growth of the cultivated apple, and pass on to my special province.

The flowers of the apple are perhaps the most beautiful of any tree's, so copious and so delicious to both sight and scent. The walker is frequently tempted to turn and linger near some more than usually handsome one, whose blossoms are two thirds expanded. How superior it is in these respects to the pear, whose blossoms are neither colored nor fragrant!

By the middle of July, green apples are so large as to remind us of coddling, and of the autumn. The sward is commonly strewed with little ones which fall still-born, as it were, — Nature thus thinning them for us. The Roman writer Palladius said, — " If apples are inclined to fall before their time, a stone placed in a split root will retain them." Some such notion, still surviving, may account for some of the stones which we see placed to be overgrown in the forks of trees. They have a saying in Suffolk, England, —

> " At Michaelmas time, or a little before,
> Half an apple goes to the core."

Early apples begin to be ripe about the first of August; but I think that none of them are so good to eat as some to smell. One is worth more to scent your handkerchief with than any perfume which they sell in the shops. The fragrance of some fruits is not to be forgotten, along with that of flowers. Some gnarly apple which I pick up in the road reminds me by its fragrance of all the wealth of Pomona, — carrying me forward to those days when they will be collected in golden and ruddy heaps in the orchards and about the cider-mills.

A week or two later, as you are going by orchards or gardens, especially in the evenings, you pass through a little region possessed by the fragrance of ripe apples, and thus enjoy them without price, and without robbing anybody.

There is thus about all natural products a certain volatile and ethereal quality which represents their highest value, and which cannot be vulgarized, or bought and sold. No mortal has ever enjoyed the perfect flavor of any fruit, and only the godlike among men begin to taste its ambrosial qualities. For nectar and ambrosia are only those fine flavors of every earthly fruit which our coarse palates fail to perceive, — just as we occupy the heaven of the gods without knowing it. When I see a particularly mean man carrying a load of fair and fragrant early apples to market, I seem to see a contest going on between him and his horse, on the one side, and the apples on the other, and, to my mind, the apples always gain it. Pliny says that apples are the heaviest of all things, and that the oxen begin to sweat at the mere sight of a load of them. Our driver begins to lose his load the moment he tries to transport them to where they do not belong, that is, to any but the most beautiful. Though he gets out from time to time, and feels of them, and thinks they are all there, I see the stream of their evanescent and celestial qualities going to heaven from his cart, while the pulp and skin and core only are going to market. They are not apples, but pomace. Are not these still Iduna's apples, the taste of which keeps the gods forever young? and think you that they will let

Loki or Thjassi carry them off to Jötunheim, while they grow wrinkled and gray? No, for Ragnarök, or the destruction of the gods, is not yet.

There is another thinning of the fruit, commonly near the end of August or in September, when the ground is strewn with windfalls; and this happens especially when high winds occur after rain. In some orchards you may see fully three quarters of the whole crop on the ground, lying in a circular form beneath the trees, yet hard and green, — or, if it is a hill-side, rolled far down the hill. However, it is an ill wind that blows nobody any good. All the country over, people are busy picking up the windfalls, and this will make them cheap for early apple-pies.

In October, the leaves falling, the apples are more distinct on the trees. I saw one year in a neighboring town some trees fuller of fruit than I remember to have ever seen before, small yellow apples hanging over the road. The branches were gracefully drooping with their weight, like a barberry-bush, so that the whole tree acquired a new character. Even the topmost branches, instead of standing erect, spread and drooped in all directions; and there were so many poles supporting the lower ones, that they looked like pictures of banian-trees. As an old English manuscript says, " The mo appelen the tree bereth, the more sche boweth to the folk."

Surely the apple is the noblest of fruits. Let the most beautiful or the swiftest have it. That should be the "going" price of apples.

Between the fifth and twentieth of October I see the barrels lie under the trees. And perhaps I talk with one who is selecting some choice barrels to fulfil an order. He turns a specked one over many times before he leaves it out. If I were to tell what is passing in my mind, I should say that every one was specked which he had handled; for he rubs off all the bloom, and those fugacious ethereal qualities leave it. Cool evenings prompt the farmers to make haste, and at length I see only the ladders here and there left leaning against the trees.

It would be well, if we accepted these gifts with more joy and gratitude, and did not think it enough simply to put a fresh load of compost about the tree. Some old English customs are suggestive at least. I find them described chiefly· in Brand's "Popular Antiquities." It appears that "on Christmas eve the farmers and their men in Devonshire take a large bowl of cider, with a toast in it, and carrying it in state to the orchard, they salute the apple-trees with much ceremony, in order to make them bear well the next season." This salutation consists in "throwing some of the cider about the roots of the tree, placing bits of the toast on the

branches," and then, " encircling one of the best
bearing trees in the orchard, they drink the following toast three several times : —

> ' Here's to thee, old apple-tree,
> Whence thou mayst bud, and whence thou mayst blow,
> And whence thou mayst bear apples enow !
>   Hats-full ! caps-full !
>   Bushel, bushel, sacks-full !
>   And my pockets full, too !   Hurra ! ' "

Also what was called " apple-howling " used
to be practised in various counties of England
on New-Year's eve.   A troop of boys visited the
different orchards, and, encircling the apple-trees,
repeated the following words : —

> " Stand fast, root ! bear well, top !
> Pray God send us a good howling crop :
> Every twig, apples big ;
> Every bow, apples enow ! "

" They then shout in chorus, one of the boys ac-
companying them on a cow's horn.   During this
ceremony they rap the trees with their sticks."
This is called " wassailing " the trees, and is
thought by some to be " a relic of the heathen
sacrifice to Pomona."

Herrick sings, —

> " Wassaile the trees that they may beare
> You many a plum and many a peare ;
> For more or less fruits they will bring
> As you so give them wassailing."

Our poets have as yet a better right to sing of cider than of wine; but it behooves them to sing better than English Phillips did, else they will do no credit to their Muse.

THE WILD APPLE.

So much for the more civilized apple-trees (*urbaniores*, as Pliny calls them). I love better to go through the old orchards of ungrafted apple-trees, at whatever season of the year, — so irregularly planted : sometimes two trees standing close together; and the rows so devious that you would think that they not only had grown while the owner was sleeping, but had been set out by him in a somnambulic state. The rows of grafted fruit will never tempt me to wander amid them like these. But I now, alas, speak rather from memory than from any recent experience, such ravages have been made!

Some soils, like a rocky tract called the Easterbrooks Country in my neighborhood, are so suited to the apple, that it will grow faster in them without any care, or if only the ground is broken up once a year, than it will in many places with any amount of care. The owners of this tract allow that the soil is excellent for fruit, but they say that it is so rocky that they

have not patience to plough it, and that, together with the distance, is the reason why it is
not cultivated. There are, or were recently, extensive orchards there standing without order.
Nay, they spring up wild and bear well there
in the midst of pines, birches, maples, and oaks.
I am often surprised to see rising amid these
trees the rounded tops of apple-trees glowing
with red or yellow fruit, in harmony with the
autumnal tints of the forest.

Going up the side of a cliff about the first of
November, I saw a vigorous young apple-tree,
which, planted by birds or cows, had shot up
amid the rocks and open woods there, and had
now much fruit on it, uninjured by the frosts,
when all cultivated apples were gathered. It
was a rank wild growth, with many green
leaves on it still, and made an impression of
thorniness. The fruit was hard and green, but
looked as if it would be palatable in the winter.
Some was dangling on the twigs, but more half-
buried in the wet leaves under the tree, or rolled
far down the hill amid the rocks. The owner
knows nothing of it. The day was not observed
when it first blossomed, nor when it first bore
fruit, unless by the chickadee. There was no
dancing on the green beneath it in its honor,
and now there is no hand to pluck its fruit, —
which is only gnawed by squirrels, as I per-

ceive. It has done double duty, — not only borne this crop, but each twig has grown a foot into the air. And this is *such* fruit! bigger than many berries, we must admit, and carried home will be sound and palatable next spring. What care I for Iduna's apples so long as I can get these?

When I go by this shrub thus late and hardy, and see its dangling fruit, I respect the tree, and I am grateful for Nature's bounty, even though I cannot eat it. Here on this rugged and woody hill-side has grown an apple-tree, not planted by man, no relic of a former orchard, but a natural growth, like the pines and oaks. Most fruits which we prize and use depend entirely on our care. Corn and grain, potatoes, peaches, melons, etc., depend altogether on our planting; but the apple emulates man's independence and enterprise. It is not simply carried, as I have said, but, like him, to some extent, it has migrated to this New World, and is even, here and there, making its way amid the aboriginal trees; just as the ox and dog and horse sometimes run wild and maintain themselves.

Even the sourest and crabbedest apple, growing in the most unfavorable position, suggests such thoughts as these, it is so noble a fruit.

THE CRAB.

Nevertheless, *our* wild apple is wild only like myself, perchance, who belong not to the aboriginal race here, but have strayed into the woods from the cultivated stock. Wilder still, as I have said, there grows elsewhere in this country a native and aboriginal Crab-Apple, *Malus coronaria*, " whose nature has not yet been modified by cultivation." It is found from Western New-York to Minnesota, and southward. Michaux says that its ordinary height " is fifteen or eighteen feet, but it is sometimes found twenty-five or thirty feet high," and that the large ones " exactly resemble the common apple-tree." " The flowers are white mingled with rose - color, and are collected in corymbs." They are remarkable for their delicious odor. The fruit, according to him, is about an inch and a half in diameter, and is intensely acid. Yet they make fine sweetmeats, and also cider of them. He concludes, that " if, on being cultivated, it does not yield new and palatable varieties, it will at least be celebrated for the beauty of its flowers, and for the sweetness of its perfume."

I never saw the Crab-Apple till May, 1861. I had heard of it through Michaux, but more modern botanists, so far as I know, have not treated it as of any peculiar importance. Thus it was a half-fabulous tree to me. I contemplated a pilgrimage to the " Glades," a portion of Pennsylvania where it was said to grow to perfection. I thought of sending to a nursery for it, but doubted if they had it, or would distinguish it from European varieties. At last I had occasion to go to Minnesota, and on entering Michigan I began to notice from the cars a tree with handsome rose-colored flowers. At first I thought it some variety of thorn; but it was not long before the truth flashed on me, that this was my long-sought Crab-Apple. It was the prevailing flowering shrub or tree to be seen from the cars at that season of the year, — about the middle of May. But the cars never stopped before one, and so I was launched on the bosom of the Mississippi without having touched one, experiencing the fate of Tantalus. On arriving at St. Anthony's Falls, I was sorry to be told that I was too far north for the Crab-Apple. Nevertheless I succeeded in finding it about eight miles west of the Falls; touched it and smelled it, and secured a lingering corymb of flowers for my herbarium. This must have been near its northern limit.

HOW THE WILD APPLE GROWS.

But though these are indigenous, like the Indians, I doubt whether they are any hardier than those backwoodsmen among the apple-trees, which, though descended from cultivated stocks, plant themselves in distant fields and forests, where the soil is favorable to them. I know of no trees which have more difficulties to contend with, and which more sturdily resist their foes. These are the ones whose story we have to tell. It oftentimes reads thus : —

Near the beginning of May, we notice little thickets of apple-trees just springing up in the pastures where cattle have been, — as the rocky ones of our Easterbrooks Country, or the top of Nobscot Hill, in Sudbury. One or two of these perhaps survive the drought and other accidents, — their very birthplace defending them against the encroaching grass and some other dangers, at first.

> In two years' time 't had thus
>   Reached the level of the rocks,
> Admired the stretching world,
>   Nor feared the wandering flocks.
>
> But at this tender age
>   Its sufferings began :
> There came a browsing ox
>   And cut it down a span.

This time, perhaps, the ox does not notice it amid the grass; but the next year, when it .has grown more stout, he recognizes it for a fellow-emigrant from the old country, the flavor of whose leaves and twigs he well knows; and though at first he pauses to welcome it, and express his surprise, and gets for answer, " The same cause that brought you here brought me," he nevertheless browses it again, reflecting, it may be, that he has some title to it.

Thus cut down annually, it does not despair; but, putting forth two short twigs for every one cut off, it spreads out low along the ground in the hollows or between the rocks, growing more stout and scrubby, until it forms, not a tree as yet, but a little pyramidal, stiff, twiggy mass, almost as solid and impenetrable as a rock. Some of the densest and most impenetrable clumps of bushes that I have ever seen, as well on account of the closeness and stubbornness of their branches as of their thorns, have been these wild-apple scrubs. They are more like the scrubby fir and black spruce on which you stand, and sometimes walk, on the tops of mountains, where cold is the demon they contend with, than anything else. No wonder they are prompted to grow thorns at last, to defend themselves against such foes. In their thorniness, however, there is no malice, only some malic acid.

The rocky pastures of the tract I have referred to, — for they maintain their ground best in a rocky field, — are thickly sprinkled with these little tufts, reminding you often of some rigid gray mosses or lichens, and you see thousands of little trees just springing up between them, with the seed still attached to them.

Being regularly clipped all around each year by the cows, as a hedge with shears, they are often of a perfect conical or pyramidal form, from one to four feet high, and more or less sharp, as if trimmed by the gardener's art. In the pastures on Nobscot Hill and its spurs, they make fine dark shadows when the sun is low. They are also an excellent covert from hawks for many small birds that roost and build in them. Whole flocks perch in them at night, and I have seen three robins' nests in one which was six feet in diameter.

No doubt many of these are already old trees, if you reckon from the day they were planted, but infants still when you consider their development and the long life before them. I counted the annual rings of some which were just one foot high, and as wide as high, and found that they were about twelve years old, but quite sound and thrifty! They were so low that they were unnoticed by the walker, while many of their contemporaries from the nurseries were already bearing considerable crops. But what you gain in time is perhaps in this case, too, lost in power, — that is, in the vigor of the tree. This is their pyramidal state.

The cows continue to browse them thus for twenty years or more, keeping them down and compelling them to spread, until at last they are so broad that they become their own fence, when some interior shoot, which their foes cannot reach, darts upward with joy : for it has not forgotten its high calling, and bears its own peculiar fruit in triumph.

Such are the tactics by which it finally defeats its bovine foes. Now, if you have watched the progress of a particular shrub, you will see that it is no longer a simple pyramid or cone, but that out of its apex there rises a sprig or two, growing more lustily perchance than an orchard-tree, since the plant now devotes the whole of its repressed energy to these upright parts. In a short time these become a small tree, an inverted pyramid resting on the apex of the other, so that the whole has now the form of a vast hour-glass. The spreading bottom, having served its purpose, finally disappears, and the generous tree permits the now harmless cows to come in and stand in its shade, and rub against and redden its trunk, which has grown in spite of them, and even to taste a part of its fruit, and so disperse the seed.

Thus the cows create their own shade and food; and the tree, its hour-glass being inverted, lives a second life, as it were.

It is an important question with some nowadays, whether you should trim young apple-trees as high as your nose or as high as your eyes. The ox trims them up as high as he can reach, and that is about the right height, I think.

In spite of wandering kine, and other adverse circumstances, that despised shrub, valued only by small birds as a covert and shelter from hawks, has its blossom-week at last, and in course of time its harvest, sincere, though small.

By the end of some October, when its leaves have fallen, I frequently see such a central sprig, whose progress I have watched, when I thought it had forgotten its destiny, as I had, bearing its first crop of small green or yellow or rosy fruit, which the cows cannot get at over the bushy and thorny hedge which surrounds it, and I make haste to taste the new and undescribed variety. We have all heard of the numerous varieties of fruit invented by Van Mons and Knight. This is the system of Van Cow, and she has invented far more and more memorable varieties than both of them.

Through what hardships it may attain to bear a sweet fruit! Though somewhat small, it may prove equal, if not superior, in flavor to that which has grown in a garden, — will perchance be all the sweeter and more palatable for the very difficulties it has had to contend with. Who knows but this chance wild fruit, planted by a cow or a bird on some remote and rocky hillside, where it is as yet unobserved by man, may be the choicest of all its kind, and foreign potentates shall hear of it, and royal societies seek to propagate it, though the virtues of the perhaps truly crabbed owner of the soil may never be heard of, — at least, beyond the limits of his village? It was thus the Porter and the Baldwin grew.

Every wild-apple shrub excites our expectation thus, somewhat as every wild child. It is, perhaps, a prince in disguise. What a lesson to man! So are human beings, referred to the highest standard, the celestial fruit which they suggest and aspire to bear, browsed on by fate; and only the most persistent and strongest genius defends itself and prevails, sends a tender scion upward at last, and drops its perfect fruit on the ungrateful earth. Poets and philosophers and statesmen thus spring up in the country pastures, and outlast the hosts of unoriginal men.

Such is always the pursuit of knowledge. The celestial fruits, the golden apples of the Hesperides, are ever guarded by a hundred-headed dragon which never sleeps, so that it is an Herculean labor to pluck them.

This is one, and the most remarkable way, in which the wild apple is propagated; but commonly it springs up at wide intervals in woods and swamps, and by the sides of roads, as the soil may suit it, and grows with comparative rapidity. Those which grow in dense woods are very tall and slender. I frequently pluck from these trees a perfectly mild and tamed fruit. As Palladius says, " *Et injussu consternitur ubere mali* ": And the ground is strewn with the fruit of an unbidden apple-tree.

It is an old notion, that, if these wild trees do not bear a valuable fruit of their own, they are the best stocks by which to transmit to posterity the most highly prized qualities of others. However, I am not in search of stocks, but the wild fruit itself, whose fierce gust has suffered no " inteneration." It is not my

> " highest plot
> To plant the Bergamot."

THE FRUIT, AND ITS FLAVOR.

The time for wild apples is the last of October and the first of November. They then get to be palatable, for they ripen late, and they are still perhaps as beautiful as ever. I make a great account of these fruits, which the farmers do not think it worth the while to gather, — wild flavors of the Muse, vivacious and inspiriting. The farmer thinks that he has better in his barrels, but he is mistaken, unless he has a walker's appetite and imagination, neither of which can he have.

Such as grow quite wild, and are left out till the first of November, I presume that the owner does not mean to gather. They belong to children as wild as themselves, — to certain active boys that I know, — to the wild-eyed woman of the fields, to whom nothing comes amiss, who gleans after all the world, — and, moreover, to us walkers. We have met with them, and they are ours. These rights, long enough insisted upon, have come to be an institution in some old countries, where they have learned how to live. I hear that "the custom of grippling, which may be called apple-gleaning, is, or was formerly, practised in Herefordshire. It consists in leaving a few apples, which are called the gripples, on every tree, after the general gathering, for the boys, who go with climbing-poles and bags to collect them."

As for those I speak of, I pluck them as a wild fruit, native to this quarter of the earth, — fruit of old trees that have been dying ever since I was a boy and are not yet dead, frequented only by the woodpecker and the squirrel, deserted now by the owner, who has not faith enough to look under their boughs. From the appearance of the tree-top, at a little distance, you would expect nothing but lichens to drop from it, but your faith is rewarded by finding the ground strewn with spirited fruit, — some of it, perhaps, collected at squirrel-holes, with the marks of their teeth by which they carried them, — some containing a cricket or two silently feeding within, and some, especially in damp days, a shelless snail. The very sticks and stones lodged in the tree-top might have convinced you of the savoriness of the fruit which has been so eagerly sought after in past years.

I have seen no account of these among the "Fruits and Fruit-Trees of America," though they are more memorable to my taste than the grafted kinds; more racy and wild American flavors do they possess, when October and November, when December and January, and perhaps February and March even, have assuaged them somewhat. An old farmer in my neighborhood, who always selects the right word, says that "they have a kind of bow-arrow tang."

Apples for grafting appear to have been selected commonly, not so much for their spirited flavor, as for their mildness, their size, and bearing qualities, — not so much for their beauty, as for their fairness and soundness. Indeed, I have no faith in the selected lists of pomological gentlemen. Their " Favorites " and " None-suches " and " Seek-no-farthers," when I have fruited them, commonly turn out very tame and forgetable. They are eaten with comparatively little zest, and have no real *tang* nor *smack* to them.

What if some of these wildings are acrid and puckery, genuine *verjuice*, do they not still belong to the *Pomaceæ*, which are uniformly innocent and kind to our race? I still begrudge them to the cider-mill. Perhaps they are not fairly ripe yet.

No wonder that these small and high-colored apples are thought to make the best cider. Loudon quotes from the " Herefordshire Report," that " apples of a small size are always, if equal in quality, to be preferred to those of a larger size, in order that the rind and kernel may bear the greatest proportion to the pulp, which affords the weakest and most watery juice." And he says, that, " to prove this, Dr. Symonds, of Hereford, about the year 1800, made one hogshead of cider entirely from the rinds and cores of apples, and another from the pulp only, when the first was found of extraordinary strength and flavor, while the latter was sweet and insipid."

Evelyn says that the " Red-strake " was the

favorite cider-apple in his day; and he quotes one Dr. Newburg as saying, " In Jersey 't is a general observation, as I hear, that the more of red any apple has in its rind, the more proper it is for this use. Pale-faced apples they exclude as much as may be from their cider-vat." This opinion still prevails.

All apples are good in November. Those which the farmer leaves out as unsalable, and unpalatable to those who frequent the markets, are choicest fruit to the walker. But it is re-markable that the wild apple, which I praise as so spirited and racy when eaten in the fields or woods, being brought into the house, has fre-quently a harsh and crabbed taste. The Saun-terer's Apple not even the saunterer can eat in the house. The palate rejects it there, as it does haws and acorns, and demands a tamed one; for there you miss the November air, which is the sauce it is to be eaten with. Accordingly, when Tityrus, seeing the lengthening shadows, invites Melibœus to go home and pass the night with him, he promises him *mild* apples and soft chest-nuts, — *mitia poma, castaneæ molles.* I fre-quently pluck wild apples of so rich and spicy a flavor that I wonder all orchardists do not get a scion from that tree, and I fail not to bring home my pockets full. But perchance, when I take one out of my desk and taste it in my chamber,

I find it unexpectedly crude, — sour enough to set a squirrel's teeth on edge and make a jay scream.

These apples have hung in the wind and frost and rain till they have absorbed the qualities of the weather or season, and thus are highly *seasoned*, and they *pierce* and *sting* and *permeate* us with their spirit. They must be eaten in *season*, accordingly, — that is, out-of-doors.

To appreciate the wild and sharp flavors of these October fruits, it is necessary that you be breathing the sharp October or November air. The out-door air and exercise which the walker gets give a different tone to his palate, and he craves a fruit which the sedentary would call harsh and crabbed. They must be eaten in the fields, when your system is all aglow with exercise, when the frosty weather nips your fingers, the wind rattles the bare boughs or rustles the few remaining leaves, and the jay is heard screaming around. What is sour in the house a bracing walk makes sweet. Some of these apples might be labelled, " To be eaten in the wind."

Of course no flavors are thrown away; they are intended for the taste that is up to them. Some apples have two distinct flavors, and perhaps one-half of them must be eaten in the house, the other out-doors. One Peter Whitney wrote from Northborough in 1782, for the Proceedings of the Boston Academy, describing an apple-tree in that town " producing fruit of opposite qualities, part of the same apple being frequently sour and the other sweet;" also some all sour, and others all sweet, and this diversity on all parts of the tree.

There is a wild apple on Nawshawtuck Hill in my town which has to me a peculiarly pleasant bitter tang, not perceived till it is three-quarters tasted. It remains on the tongue. As you eat it, it smells exactly like a squash-bug. It is a sort of triumph to eat and relish it.

I hear that the fruit of a kind of plum-tree in Provence is " called *Prunes sibarelles*, because it is impossible to whistle after having eaten them, from their sourness." But perhaps they were only eaten in the house and in summer, and if tried out-of-doors in a stinging atmosphere, who knows but you could whistle an octave higher and clearer ?

In the fields only are the sours and bitters of Nature appreciated; just as the wood-chopper eats his meal in a sunny glade, in the middle of a winter day, with content, basks in a sunny ray there and dreams of summer in a degree of cold which, experienced in a chamber, would make a student miserable. They who are at work abroad are not cold, but rather it is they who sit shivering in houses. As with temperatures, so with flavors; as with cold and heat, so with sour and sweet. This natural raciness, the sours and bitters which the diseased palate refuses, are the true condiments.

Let your condiments be in the condition of your senses. To appreciate the flavor of these wild apples requires vigorous and healthy senses, *papillæ* firm and erect on the tongue and palate, not easily flattened and tamed.

From my experience with wild apples, I can understand that there may be reason for a savage's preferring many kinds of food which the civilized man rejects. The former has the palate of an out-door man. It takes a savage or wild taste to appreciate a wild fruit.

What a healthy out-of-door appetite it takes to relish the apple of life, the apple of the world, then !

> " Nor is it every apple I desire,
>   Nor that which pleases every palate best ;
> 'T is not the lasting Deuxan I require,
>   Nor yet the red-cheeked Greening I request,
> Nor that which first beshrewed the name of wife,
> Nor that whose beauty caused the golden strife :
> No, nö ! bring me an apple from the tree of life."

So there is one *thought* for the field, another for the house. I would have my thoughts, like wild apples, to be food for walkers, and will not warrant them to be palatable, if tasted in the house.

THEIR BEAUTY.

Almost all wild apples are handsome. They cannot be too gnarly and crabbed and rusty to look at. The gnarliest will have some redeeming traits even to the eye. You will discover some evening redness dashed or sprinkled on some protuberance or in some cavity. It is rare that the summer lets an apple go without streaking or spotting it on some part of its sphere. It will have some red stains, commemorating the mornings and evenings it has witnessed; some dark and rusty blotches, in memory of the clouds and foggy, mildewy days that have passed over it; and a spacious field of green reflecting the general face of Nature, — green even as the fields; or a yellow ground, which implies a milder flavor, — yellow as the harvest, or russet as the hills.

Apples, these I mean, unspeakably fair, — apples not of Discord, but of Concord! Yet not so rare but that the homeliest may have a share. Painted by the frosts, some a uniform clear bright yellow, or red, or crimson, as if their spheres had regularly revolved, and enjoyed the influence of the sun on all sides alike, — some with the faintest pink blush imaginable, — some brindled with deep red streaks like a cow, or with hundreds of fine blood-red rays running regularly from the stem-dimple to the blossom-end, like meridional lines, on a straw-colored ground, — some touched with a greenish rust, like a fine lichen, here and there, with crimson blotches or eyes more or less confluent and fiery when wet, — and others gnarly, and freckled or peppered all over on the stem side with fine crimson spots on a white ground, as if accidentally sprinkled from the brush of Him who paints the autumn leaves. Others, again, are sometimes red inside, perfused with a beautiful blush, fairy food, too beautiful to eat, — apple of the Hesperides, apple of the evening sky! But like shells and pebbles on the sea-shore, they must be seen as they sparkle amid the withering leaves in some dell in the woods, in the autumnal air, or as they lie in the wet grass, and not when they have wilted and faded in the house.

THE NAMING OF THEM.

It would be a pleasant pastime to find suitable names for the hundred varieties which go to a single heap at the cider-mill. Would it not tax a man's invention, — no one to be named after a man, and all in the *lingua vernacula?* Who shall stand godfather at the christening of the wild apples? It would exhaust the Latin and Greek languages, if they were used, and make the *lingua vernacula* flag. We should have to call in the sunrise and the sunset, the rainbow and the autumn woods and the wild flowers, and the woodpecker and the purple finch and the squirrel and the jay and the butterfly, the November traveller and the truant boy, to our aid.

In 1836 there were in the garden of the London Horticultural Society more than fourteen hundred distinct sorts. But here are species which they have not in their catalogue, not to mention the varieties which our Crab might yield to cultivation.

Let us enumerate a few of these. I find myself compelled, after all, to give the Latin names of some for the benefit of those who live where English is not spoken, — for they are likely to have a world-wide reputation.

There is, first of all, the Wood-Apple (*Malus sylvatica*); the Blue-Jay Apple; the Apple which grows in Dells in the Woods, (*sylvestrivallis,*) also in Hollows in Pastures (*campestrivallis*); the Apple that grows in an old Cellar-Hole (*Malus cellaris*); the Meadow-Apple; the Partridge-Apple; the Truant's Apple, (*Cessatoris,*) which no boy will ever go by without knocking off some, however *late* it may be; the Saunterer's Apple, — you must lose yourself before you can find the way to that; the Beauty of the Air (*Decus Aëris*); December-Eating; the

Frozen-Thawed (*gelato-soluta*), good only in that state; the Concord Apple, possibly the same with the *Musketaquidensis*; the Assabet Apple; the Brindled Apple; Wine of New England; the Chickaree Apple; the Green Apple (*Malus viridis*); — this has many synonymes; in an imperfect state, it is the *Cholera morbifera aut dysenterifera, puerulis dilectissima*; — the Apple which Atalanta stopped to pick up; the Hedge-Apple (*Malus Sepium*); the Slug-Apple (*limacea*); the Railroad-Apple, which perhaps came from a core thrown out of the cars; the Apple whose Fruit we tasted in our Youth; our Particular Apple, not to be found in any catalogue, — *Pedestrium Solatium*; also the Apple where hangs the Forgotten Scythe; Iduna's Apples, and the Apples which Loki found in the Wood; and a great many more I have on my list, too numerous to mention, — all of them good. As Bodæus exclaims, referring to the cultivated kinds, and adapting Virgil to his case, so I, adapting Bodæus, —

> " Not if I had a hundred tongues, a hundred mouths,
>   An iron voice, could I describe all the forms
>   And reckon up all the names of these *wild apples*."

THE LAST GLEANING.

By the middle of November the wild apples have lost some of their brilliancy, and have chiefly fallen. A great part are decayed on the ground, and the sound ones are more palatable than before. The note of the chickadee sounds now more distinct, as you wander amid the old trees, and the autumnal dandelion is half-closed and tearful. But still, if you are a skilful gleaner, you may get many a pocket-full even of grafted fruit, long after apples are supposed to be gone out-of-doors. I know a Blue-Pear-main tree, growing within the edge of a swamp, almost as good as wild. You would not suppose that there was any fruit left there, on the first survey, but you must look according to system. Those which lie exposed are quite brown and rotten now, or perchance a few still show one blooming cheek here and there amid the wet leaves. Nevertheless, with experienced eyes, I explore amid the bare alders and the huckle-berry-bushes and the withered sedge, and in the crevices of the rocks, which are full of leaves, and pry under the fallen and decaying ferns, which, with apple and alder leaves, thickly strew the ground. For I know that they lie concealed, fallen into hollows long since and covered up by the leaves of the tree itself, — a proper kind of packing. From these lurking-places, anywhere within the circumference of the tree, I draw forth the fruit, all wet and glossy, maybe nibbled by rabbits and hollowed out by crickets and per-haps with a leaf or two cemented to it (as Curzon an old manuscript from a monastery's mouldy cellar), but still with a rich bloom on it, and at least as ripe and well kept, if not better than those in barrels, more crisp and lively than they. If these resources fail to yield anything, I have learned to look between the bases of the suckers which spring thickly from some horizontal limb, for now and then one lodges there, or in the very midst of an alder-clump, where they are covered by leaves, safe from cows which may have smelled them out. If I am sharp-set, for I do not refuse the Blue-Pearmain, I fill my pockets on each side; and as I retrace my steps in the frosty eve, being perhaps four or five miles from home, I eat one first from this side, and then from that, to keep my balance.

I learn from Topsell's Gesner, whose authority appears to be Albertus, that the following is the way in which the hedgehog collects and carries home his apples. He says, — "His meat is apples, worms, or grapes: when he findeth apples or grapes on the earth, he rolleth himself upon them, until he have filled all his prickles, and then carrieth them home to his den, never bearing above one in his mouth; and if it fortune that one of them fall off by the way, he likewise shaketh off all the residue, and walloweth upon them afresh, until they be all settled upon his back again. So, forth he goeth, making a noise like a cart-wheel; and if he have any

young ones in his nest, they pull off his load
wherewithal he is loaded, eating thereof what
they please, and laying up the residue for the
time to come."

THE "FROZEN-THAWED" APPLE.

Toward the end of November, though some
of the sound ones are yet more mellow and
perhaps more edible, they have generally, like
the leaves, lost their beauty, and are beginning
to freeze.   It is finger-cold, and prudent farmers
get in their barrelled apples, and bring you the
apples and cider which they have engaged; for
it is time to put them into the cellar.   Perhaps
a few on the ground show their red cheeks
above the early snow, and occasionally some
even preserve their color and soundness under
the snow throughout the winter.   But generally
at the beginning of the winter they freeze hard,
and soon, though undecayed, acquire the color
of a baked apple.

Before the end of December, generally, they
experience their first thawing.   Those which a
month ago were sour, crabbed, and quite unpalatable to the civilized taste, such at least as
were frozen while sound, let a warmer sun come
to thaw them, for they are extremely sensitive
to its rays, are found to be filled with a rich,

sweet cider, better than any bottled cider that I know of, and with which I am better acquainted than with wine. All apples are good in this state, and your jaws are the cider-press. Others, which have more substance, are a sweet and luscious food, — in my opinion of more worth than the pine-apples which are imported from the West Indies. Those which lately even I tasted only to repent of it, — for I am semi-civilized, — which the farmer willingly left on the tree, I am now glad to find have the property of hanging on like the leaves of the young oaks. It is a way to keep cider sweet without boiling. Let the frost come to freeze them first, solid as stones, and then the rain or a warm winter day to thaw them, and they will seem to have borrowed a flavor from heaven through the medium of the air in which they hang. Or perchance you find, when you get home, that those which rattled in your pocket have thawed, and the ice is turned to cider. But after the third or fourth freezing and thawing they will not be found so good.

What are the imported half-ripe fruits of the torrid South, to this fruit matured by the cold of the frigid North? These are those crabbed apples with which I cheated my companion, and kept a smooth face that I might tempt him to eat. Now we both greedily fill our pockets

with them, — bending to drink the cup and save
our lappets from the overflowing juice, — and
grow more social with their wine. Was there
one that hung so high and sheltered by the
tangled branches that our sticks could not dis-
lodge it?

It is a fruit never carried to market, that I
am aware of, — quite distinct from the apple
of the markets, as from dried apple and cider,
— and it is not every winter that produces it in
perfection.

The era of the Wild Apple will soon be past.
It is a fruit which will probably become extinct
in New England. You may still wander through
old orchards of native fruit of great extent, which
for the most part went to the cider-mill, now all
gone to decay. I have heard of an orchard in
a distant town, on the side of a hill, where the
apples rolled down and lay four feet deep
against a wall on the lower side, and this the
owner cut down for fear they should be made
into cider. Since the temperance reform and
the general introduction of grafted fruit, no
native apple-trees, such as I see everywhere in
deserted pastures, and where the woods have
grown up around them, are set out. I fear that
he who walks over these fields a century hence
will not know the pleasure of knocking off

wild apples. Ah, poor man, there are many pleasures which he will not know! Notwithstanding the prevalence of the Baldwin and the Porter, I doubt if so extensive orchards are set out to-day in my town as there were a century ago, when those vast straggling cider-orchards were planted, when men both ate and drank apples, when the pomace-heap was the only nursery, and trees cost nothing but the trouble of setting them out. Men could afford then to stick a tree by every wall-side and let it take its chance. I see nobody planting trees to-day in such out-of-the-way places, along the lonely roads and lanes, and at the bottom of dells in the wood. Now that they have grafted trees, and pay a price for them, they collect them into a plat by their houses, and fence them in, — and the end of it all will be that we shall be, compelled to look for our apples in a barrel.

This is " The word of the Lord that came to Joel the son of Pethuel.

" Hear this, ye old men, and give ear, all ye inhabitants of the land! Hath this been in your days, or even in the days of your fathers ? . . . .

" That which the palmer-worm hath left hath the locust eaten ; and that which the locust hath left hath the canker-worm eaten; and that which the canker-worm hath left hath the caterpillar eaten.

"Awake, ye drunkards, and weep! and howl, all ye drinkers of wine, because of the new wine! for it is cut off from your mouth.

"For a nation is come up upon my land, strong, and without number, whose teeth are the teeth of a lion, and he hath the cheek-teeth of a great lion.

"He hath laid my vine waste, and barked my fig-tree; he hath made it clean bare, and cast it away; the branches thereof are made white. . . . .

"Be ye ashamed, O ye husbandmen! howl, O ye vine-dressers! . . . .

"The vine is dried up, and the fig-tree languisheth; the pomegranate-tree, the palm-tree also, and the apple-tree, even all the trees of the field, are withered: because joy is withered away from the sons of men."

Other Applewood Books You Might Enjoy

The Gospel of Nature
by John Burroughs

In 1912, America's great naturalist John Burroughs was asked by a preacher to talk to his congregation on the "gospel of Nature." In this response, Burroughs focused on what gave him solace and strength. Today, *The Gospel of Nature* has lived on as a powerfully moving message of people's relationship to the infinite forces of Nature.

ISBN: 1-55709-131-5   **paperback**   **$5.95**

Stickeen
Story of a Dog
by John Muir

The touching story of how John Muir came to know and love Stickeen, a half-wild dog, whom he met while on a river trip through Alaska.

ISBN: 1-55709-112-9   **cloth**   **$7.95**

Walking
by Henry David Thoreau

Walking, now again considered to be an important form of exercise, was the activity from which Thoreau examined humankind's relationship with nature in this famous essay.

ISBN:1-55709-100-5   **paperback**   **$5.95**

Applewood Books are available from your Bookseller
or directly from:
The Globe Pequot Press, Box Q, Chester, CT 06412• (203) 526-9571